LETTERS ARE CHARACTERS

COLORING & MULTISENSORY ACTIVITY BOOK

A Play-Based, Reading Program For Emerging Readers And
An Essential Reading Curriculum for Caregivers

Caroline Wilcox Ugurlu, PHD

Outskirts Press, Inc.
http://www.outskirtspress.com

ISBN: 978-1-9772-3608-1

Illustrations by Caroline Wilcox Ugurlu, Ph.D.
Author Photo © 2021 Terry Augustyn, Nutmeg Photography.
All rights reserved – used with permission.

Outskirts Press and the "OP" logo are trademarks belonging to Outskirts Press, Inc.

PRINTED IN THE UNITED STATES OF AMERICA

This book is dedicated to Samantha and AJ.

It is for emerging readers everywhere, those who struggle and those who don't. Keep reading, and always bring a book along. Read deeply and often to strengthen your empathy. The world needs your empathy and understanding.

It is also for parents and caregivers. You are your children's first and most important teachers. You make all the difference. Know that for a child who is struggling to read, the issue is not that they need to try harder; it is that adults need to teach them in a way that they can learn.

Dear Parents and Caregivers,

So often parents and caregivers tell me stories about their children's experiences with learning to read. Very often, these stories are joyful. It clicks and the child starts a lifelong love affair with books. Just as often, the stories are of struggles, deep pain, and diminished self-esteem. This bears out in the numbers: 20 to 25 percent of children will struggle when they learn to read. Two-thirds of fourth graders are not reaching fluency benchmarks. The hope and truth is that almost every child can learn to read at an average or better level if taught in a way that they can learn. Helping kids early is the way to go, so spread the word. Multisensory repetitive, play-based, explicit, scaffolded instruction works for all children. This is the reason I created Letters are Characters©. I want to reach as many parents and caregivers as possible because you, more than anyone, make the difference in the life of a child. You are the constant in their life. Awareness and understanding will ensure that your child reads to his or her highest potential.

This multisensory coloring/activity book contains engaging and purposeful play-based activities. Experiment with the ones that resonate with your child. Consider working on one letter a week if you are just starting. If your learner already knows some letters, you can target the ones that are most difficult. Follow your child's lead as they make the letters their own. Use letter dough or clay to make letters on top of the letters they color, beside the letters, and eventually without the letters.

This multisensory coloring/activity book is the workbook that goes along with the Letters are Characters© companion hardcover book. I hope that you enjoy the process of starting your child on the road to be a great reader. It is one of the best gifts that you can give and affords many protections. It is also so much fun. When your child reads his or her first words, it is magical. Enjoy the journey.

Warmly,
Caroline Wilcox Ugurlu, PhD, WDP
Author and Creator of Letters are Characters©

P.S. You will note that some sounds are separated with hyphens (b-b-b) in order to indicate a consecutive production of a noncontinuous sound. Other sounds, such as aaa or sss, do not have hyphens because they are continuous sounds.

SMELL

- Choose a scent for A, a, a. Would they smell like aaapples, apricots, or anchovies?

TOUCH

- Touch the A, a, a in your coloring book. Trace the letter with your fingers.
- Build the letter with letter dough or clay.
- Make the letter in shaving cream or blocks!

MOVEMENT

- Skywrite the letter. Extend your arm with a straight elbow; point your pointer and middle finger and use them to write the letter in the air!
- Lie down on the floor and try to make the letter shapes! Use props if you need them. Have someone take a picture. Look at it and see how you did.

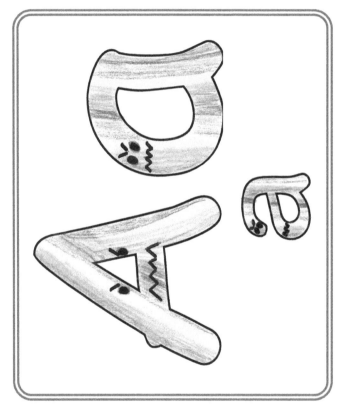

VISION

- Look at A and babies a, a. Study the shapes.
- Make them rainbow colors because they are vowels. All vowels have a long sound (their name) and a short sound!
- Make their faces look angry!

HEARING

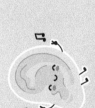

- Hear the sounds Ā (letter name) and ă (a, at).
- Try saying: "A let me aaat 'em! I want to be first!"
- Put your hand on your neck and feel the vibration in your vocal cords. Vowel sounds are made with your vocal cords.

TASTE

- Taste foods that A, a, a might like. Say the sound right before you try a bite. You can try apples, apricots, or asparagus.

SMELL

- Choose a scent for B, b. Would they smell like b-b-bananas, bread, blueberries, or broccoli?

TOUCH

- Touch the B, b in your coloring book. Trace the letter with your fingers.
- Build the letter with letter dough or clay.
- Make the letter in shaving cream or blocks!

MOVEMENT

- Skywrite the letter. Extend your arm with a straight elbow; point your pointer and middle finger and use them to write the letter in the air!
- Lie down on the floor and try to make the letter shapes! Use props if you need them. Have someone take a picture. Look at it and see how you did.

VISION

- Look at B and baby b. Study the shapes. Baby b likes to sit on her mom's belly!
- Make B, b one color because they only make one sound.
- Add lines below them to make them bounce!

HEARING

- Hear the sound b-b-b-bounce!
- Feel how the sound is made by a force of air pushed through your lips.
- Jump up and down saying/hearing the b-b-b sound as you b-b-bounce.

TASTE

- Taste foods that B, b might like. Say the sound right before you try a bite. You can try bananas, broccoli, or butter.

SMELL

- Choose a scent for C, c. Would they smell like carrots, cake, or celery?

TOUCH

- Touch the C, c in your coloring book. Trace the letter with your fingers.
- Build the letter with letter dough or clay.
- Make the letter in shaving cream or blocks!

MOVEMENT

- Skywrite the letter. Extend your arm with a straight elbow; point your pointer and middle finger and use them to write the letter in the air!
- Lie down on the floor and try to make the letter shapes! Use props if you need them. Have someone take a picture. Look at it and see how you did.

VISION

- Look at C and baby c. Study the shapes.
- Color them two colors because they have two sounds. Since one sounds like s, make his hair look like little sss. C sounds like s when he sits next to e, i or y and like k when he sits next to a, o, or u.
- Make cute faces!

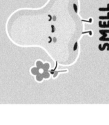

HEARING

- Hear the sounds C makes (K and S) c-c-carrots and cccelery. C likes to curve.
- Notice how the two sounds are made in your mouth. The hard c sound (k) is made with a force of air and your tongue position. The soft c (s) sound is made by forcing air through your teeth.

TASTE

- Taste foods that C, c might like. Say the sound right before you try a bite. You can try celery, carrots, carrot cake, cupcakes, or cilantro.

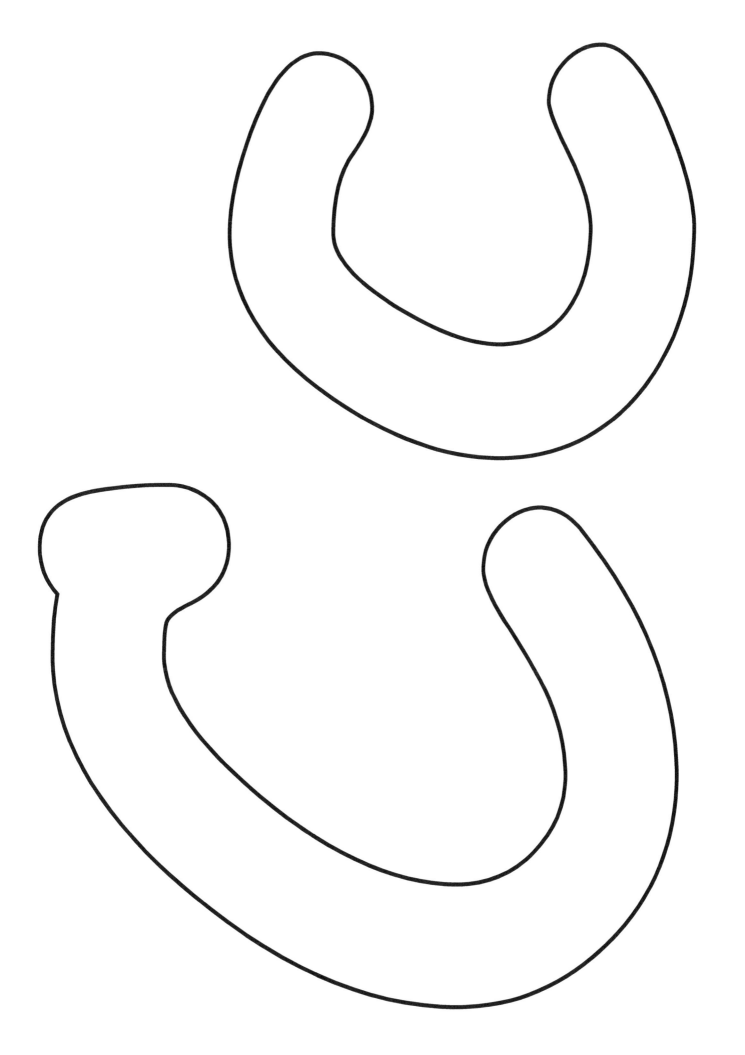

VISION

- Look at D and baby d. Study the shapes. Baby d likes to have c jump on to go for a ride... c...d. Picture that! This may help kids tell b and d apart!
- Make D, d one color because they only make one sound. Make them capes because they are a daring duo.
- Draw brave faces!

SMELL

- Choose a scent for D, d. Would they smell like doughnuts, deviled eggs, dip, or dumplings?

TOUCH

- Touch the D, d in your coloring book. Trace the letter with your fingers.
- Build the letter with letter dough or clay.
- Make the letter in shaving cream or blocks!

HEARING

- Hear the sound d-d-d-daring!
- Feel how the sound is made by a force of air while your tongue moves away from the roof of your mouth.

MOVEMENT

- Skywrite the letter. Extend your arm with a straight elbow; point your pointer and middle finger and use them to write the letter in the air!
- Lie down on the floor and try to make the letter shapes! Use props if you need them. Have someone take a picture. Look at it and see how you did.

TASTE

- Taste foods that D, d might like. Say the sound right before you try a bite. You can try doughnuts, dough, or dates.

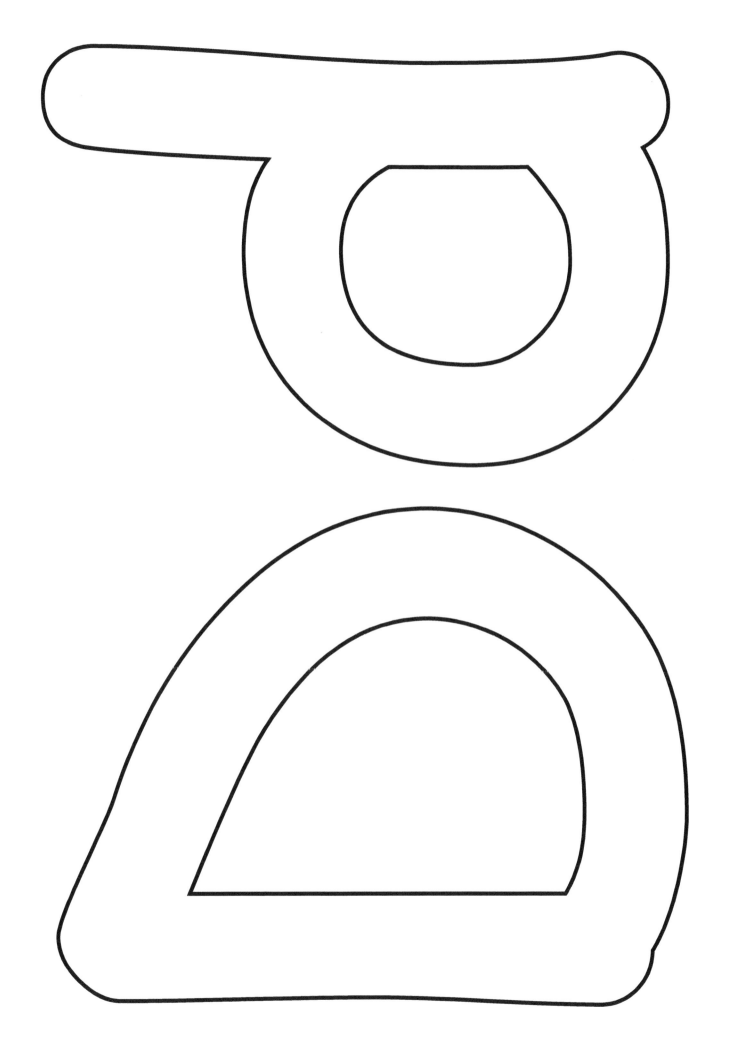

SMELL

- Choose a scent for E, e! Would they smell like eggs, English muffins, or eclairs?

TOUCH

- Touch the E, e in your coloring book. Trace the letter with your fingers.
- Build the letter with letter dough or clay.
- Make the letter in shaving cream or blocks!

MOVEMENT

- Skywrite the letter. Extend your arm with a straight elbow; point your pointer and middle finger and use them to write the letter in the air!
- Lie down on the floor and try to make the letter shapes! Use props if you need them. Have someone take a picture. Look at it and see how you did.

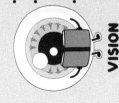

VISION

- Look at E and baby e. Study the shapes.
- Make them rainbow colors because they are vowels. All vowels have a long sound (their name) and a short sound!
- Make two versions – one that looks scared (and squeals EEE!) and one that looks brave! When e sits at the end of a consonant-vowel-consonant-e pattern word, he is brave and quiet so that the vowel in the middle can say his long sound. Brav (nonsense word) becomes Brave!!

HEARING

- Hear the sounds Ē (letter name) and ĕ (eeegg). E says: "I am eeeager to help! I will help other vowels say their long sound by sitting at the eeend of the word."
- Put your hand on your neck and feel the vibration in your vocal cords.
- Vowel sounds are made with your vocal cords.

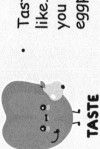

TASTE

- Taste foods that E, e might like. Say the sound right before you try a bite. You can try eggs, eggplant, edamame, or eclairs.

SMELL

SMELL

- Choose a scent for F, f. Would they smell like flowers or french fries?

TOUCH

TOUCH

- Touch the F, f in your coloring book. Trace the letter with your fingers.
- Build the letter with letter dough or clay.
- Make the letter in shaving cream or blocks!

MOVEMENT

MOVEMENT

- Skywrite the letter. Extend your arm with a straight elbow, point your pointer and middle finger and use them to write the letter in the air!
- Lie down on the floor and try to make the letter shapes! Use props if you need them. Have someone take a picture. Look at it and see how you did.

VISION

VISION

- Look at F and baby f. Study the shapes. F can fly so make a cape! Make F, f one color because they only make one sound.

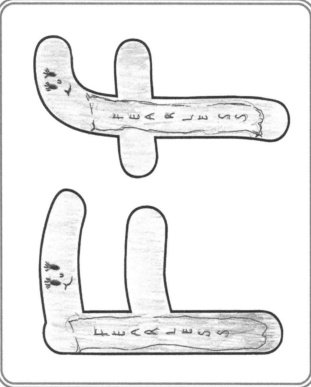

HEARING

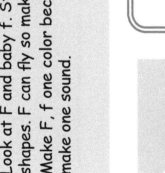

HEARING

- Hear the sound ffffly!
- Feel how the sound is made when you put your top teeth on your bottom lip and blow.
- Whisper the sound and then try to say it loudly. When you say it loudly, does it turn into another sound? (Hint: It sounds like V!)

TASTE

TASTE

- Taste foods that F, f might like. Say the sound right before you try a bite. You can try french fries, feta, fish, or figs.

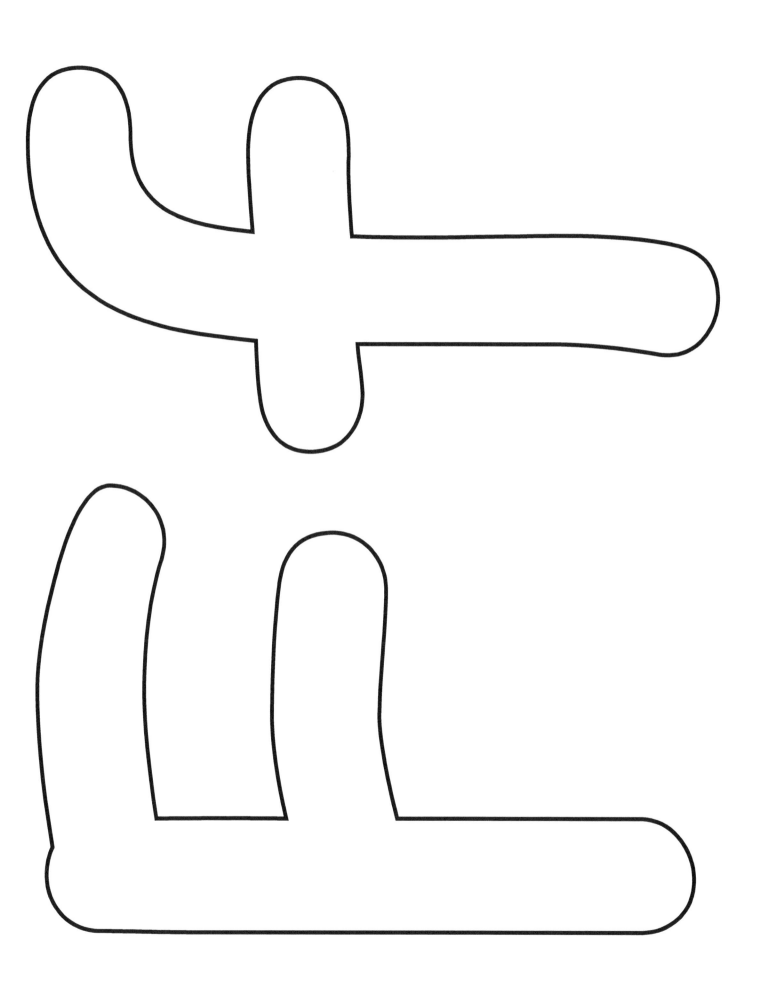

SMELL

- Choose a scent for G, g. Would they smell like grapes or hair gel?

VISION

- Look at G and baby g. Study the shapes.
- Make them two colors because they have two sounds. G (usually) sounds like soft g (gel) when he sits next to e, i, or y and like hard g (gut) when he sits next to a, o, or u.
- Make faces that look generous, giving, and giggly.

TOUCH

- Touch the G, g in your coloring book. Trace the letter with your fingers.
- Build the letter with letter dough or clay.
- Make the letter in shaving cream or blocks!

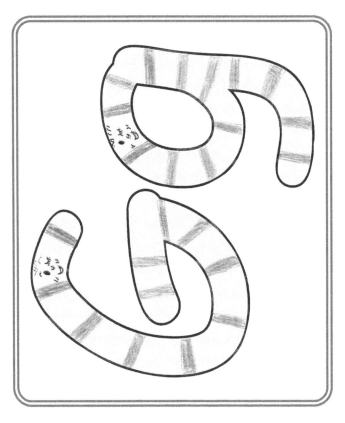

HEARING

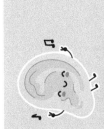

- Hear the sounds G, g (Gut, Gel – like a J).
- Notice how the two sounds are made in your mouth. The hard g sound is made in the back of your throat. The soft g sound is the same as j and it's made by a force of air when your tongue is up near the roof of your mouth (you can't feel it in your throat).

MOVEMENT

- Skywrite the letter. Extend your arm with a straight elbow; point your pointer and middle finger and use them to write the letter in the air!
- Lie down on the floor and try to make the letter shapes! Use props if you need them. Have someone take a picture. Look at it and see how you did.

TASTE

- Taste foods that G, g might like. Say the sound right before you try a bite. You can try grapes, grapefruit, greens, garlic, or gum.

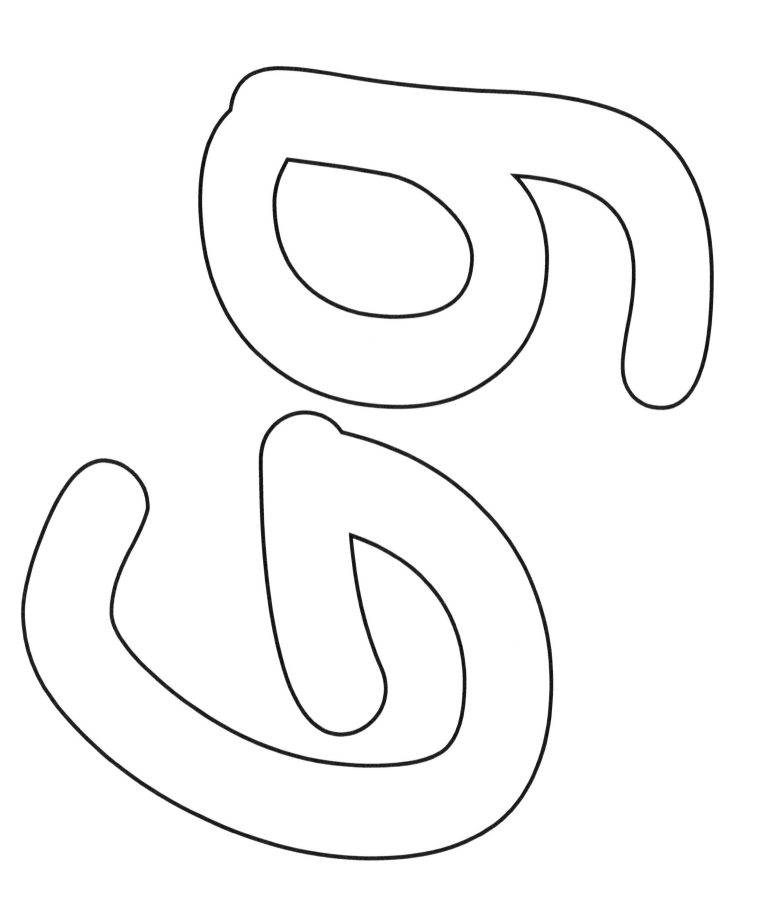

VISION

- Look at H and baby h. Study the shapes. Baby h looks like her mom without her top line. Maybe she will grow it when she gets older!
- Make H, h one color because they only make one sound. Make happy faces!

SMELL

- Choose a scent for H, h. Would they smell like hamburgers, hot dogs, or happiness? What does happiness smell like to you?

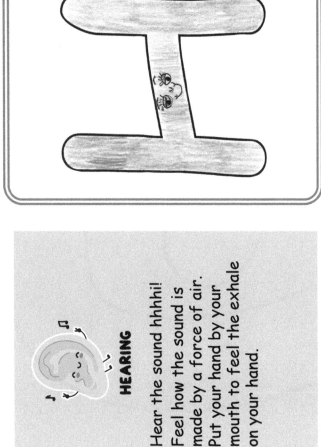

TOUCH

- Touch the H, h in your coloring book. Trace the letter with your fingers.
- Build the letter with letter dough or clay.
- Make the letter in shaving cream or blocks!

HEARING

- Hear the sound hhhh!
- Feel how the sound is made by a force of air. Put your hand by your mouth to feel the exhale on your hand.

MOVEMENT

- Skywrite the letter. Extend your arm with a straight elbow; point your pointer and middle finger and use them to write the letter in the air!
- Lie down on the floor and try to make the letter shapes! Use props if you need them. Have someone take a picture. Look at it and see how you did.

TASTE

- Taste foods that H, h might like. Say the sound right before you try a bite. You can try hamburger, honey, honeydew, ham, or hummus.

Choose a scent for I, i. Would they smell (stink) like ink?

SMELL

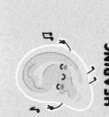

TOUCH

- Touch the I, i in your coloring book. Trace the letter with your fingers.
- Build the letter with letter dough or clay.
- Make the letter in shaving cream or blocks!

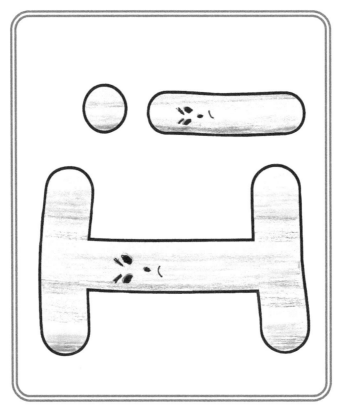

MOVEMENT

- Skywrite the letter. Extend your arm with a straight elbow; point your pointer and middle finger and use them to write the letter in the air!
- Lie down on the floor and try to make the letter shapes! Use props if you need them. Have someone take a picture. Look at it and see how you did.

VISION

- Look at I and baby i. Study the shapes
- Make them rainbow colors because they are vowels. All vowels have a long sound (their name) and a short sound!
- Make their faces intense (that means serious)!

HEARING

- Hear the sounds Ī (letter name) and ĭ (iiit) "I am iiinteresting!"
- Put your hand on your neck and feel the vibration in your vocal cords.
- Vowel sounds are made with your vocal cords.

TASTE

- Taste foods that I, i might like. Say the sound right before you try a bite. You can try, "I have an iiitch for iiice cream."

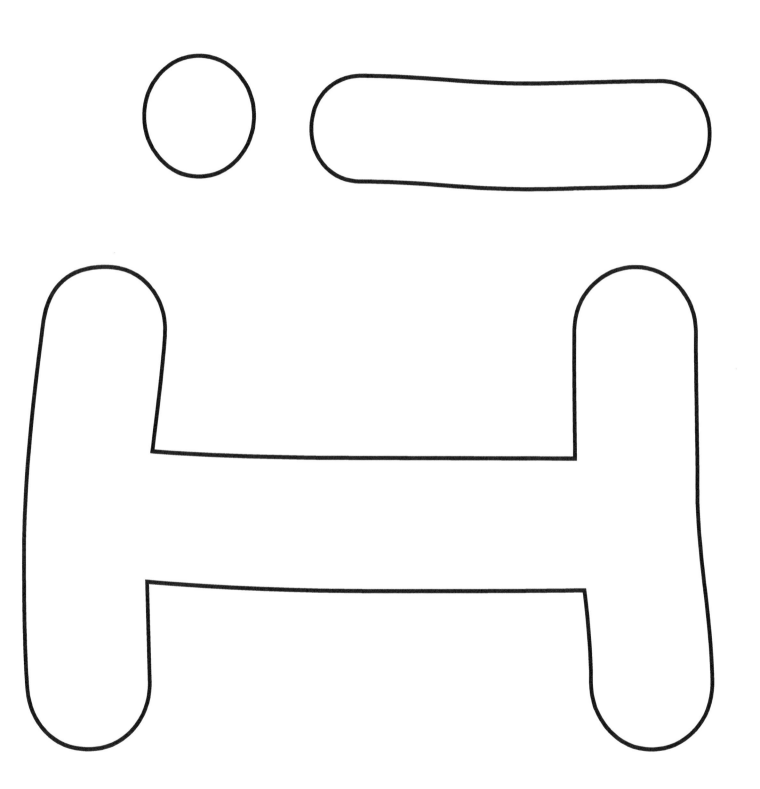

VISION

- Look at J and baby j. Study the shapes.
- Make J, j one color because they only make one sound.
- Make jolly (that means happy) pirate faces!

SMELL

- Choose a scent for J, j. Would they smell like java (coffee) or jellybeans?

TOUCH

- Touch the J, j in your coloring book. Trace the letter with your fingers.
- Build the letter with letter dough or clay.
- Make the letter in shaving cream or blocks!

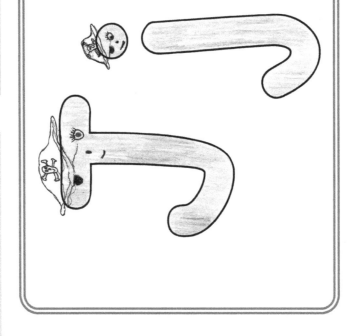

HEARING

- Hear the sound j-j-j-jar.
- Feel how the sound is made by a force of air when your tongue is up near the roof of your mouth.

MOVEMENT

- Skywrite the letter. Extend your arm with a straight elbow; point your pointer and middle finger and use them to write the letter in the air!
- Lie down on the floor and try to make the letter shapes! Use props if you need them. Have someone take a picture. Look at it and see how you did.

TASTE

- Taste foods that J, j might like. Say the sound right before you try a bite. You can try jam, jelly, Jell-O, jerky, or juice.

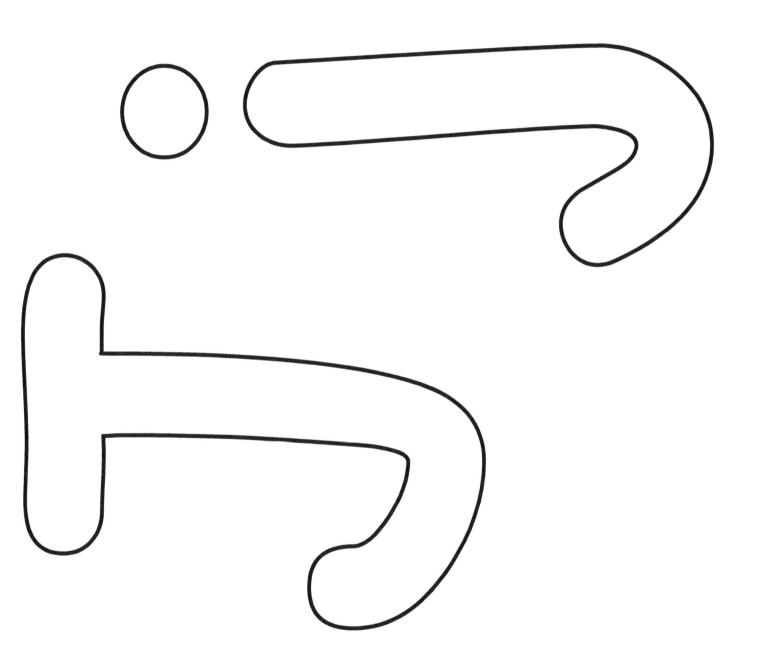

SMELL

- Choose a scent for K, k. Would they smell like kale, kebabs, or kindergarten?

TOUCH

- Touch the K, k in your coloring book. Trace the letter with your fingers.
- Build the letter with letter dough or clay.
- Make the letter in shaving cream or blocks!

MOVEMENT

- Skywrite the letter. Extend your arm with a straight elbow; point your pointer and middle finger and use them to write the letter in the air!
- Lie down on the floor and try to make the letter shapes! Use props if you need them. Have someone take a picture. Look at it and see how you did.

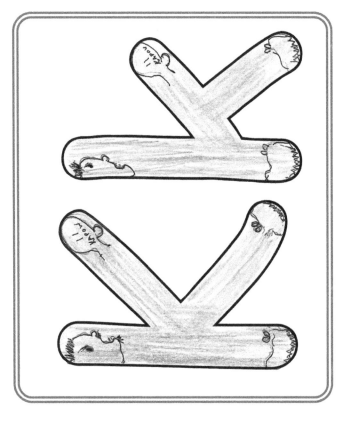

VISION

- Look at K and baby k. Study the shapes.
- Make K, k one color because they only make one sound.
- Make mean faces! K loves to kick!

HEARING

- Hear the sound k-k-k-kick.
- Feel how the sound is made in the back of your throat.

TASTE

- Taste foods that K, k might like. Say the sound right before you try a bite. You can try kebabs, kiwi, or kale.

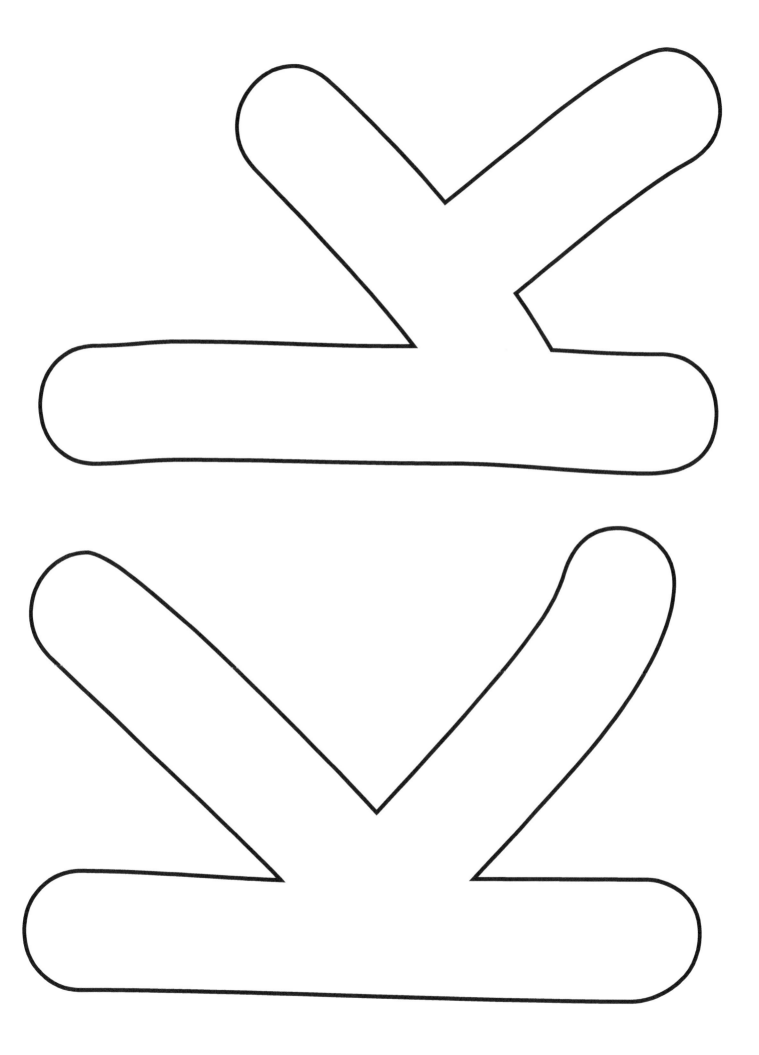

VISION

- Look at L and baby l. Study the shapes.
- Make L, l one color because they only make one sound.
- Make loving faces!

TOUCH

- Touch the L, l in your coloring book. Trace the letter with your fingers.
- Build the letter with letter dough or clay.
- Make the letter in shaving cream or blocks!

SMELL

- Choose a scent for L, l. Would they smell like lavender, lemons, or licorice?

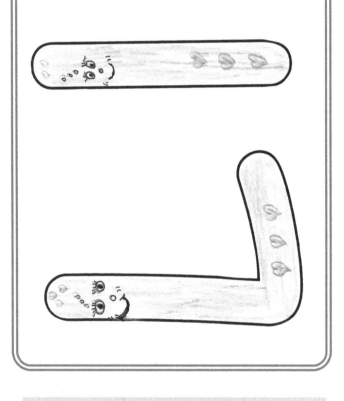

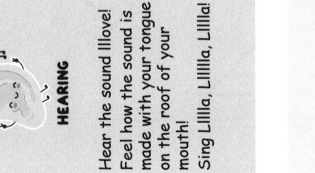

HEARING

- Hear the sound lllove!
- Feel how the sound is made with your tongue on the roof of your mouth!
- Sing Llllla, Llllla, Llllla!

MOVEMENT

- Skywrite the letter. Extend your arm with a straight elbow; point your pointer and middle finger and use them to write the letter in the air!
- Lie down on the floor and try to make the letter shapes! Use props if you need them. Have someone take a picture. Look at it and see how you did.

TASTE

- Taste foods that L, l might like. Say the sound right before you try a bite. You can try limes, lemons, licorice, lollipops, or lasagna.

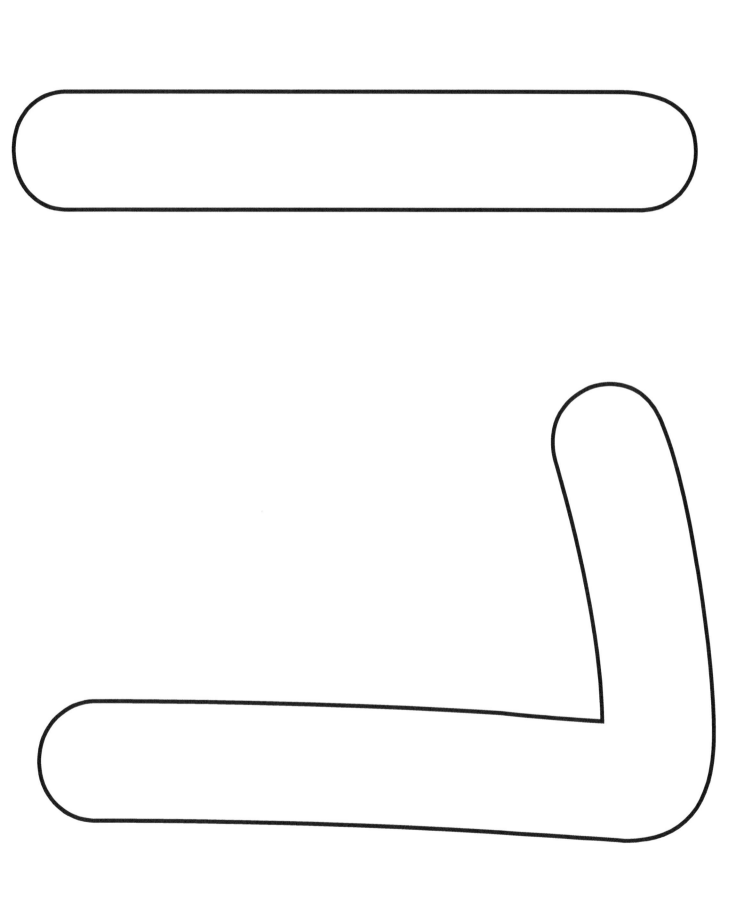

SMELL

- Choose a scent for M, m. Would they smell like mangoes, meatloaf, or milk?

TOUCH

- Touch the M, m in your coloring book. Trace the letter with your fingers.
- Build the letter with letter dough or clay.
- Make the letter in shaving cream or blocks!

MOVEMENT

- Skywrite the letter. Extend your arm with a straight elbow; point your pointer and middle finger and use them to write the letter in the air!
- Lie down on the floor and try to make the letter shapes! Use props if you need them. Have someone take a picture. Look at it and see how you did.

VISION

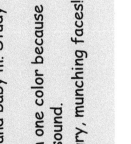

- Look at M and baby m. Study the shapes.
- Make M, m one color because they only make one sound.
- Make hungry, munching faces!

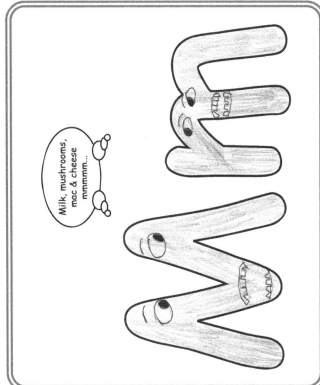

Milk, mushrooms, mac & cheese mmmmm...

HEARING

- Hear the sound mmmunch!
- Feel how the sound is made with your lips together!
- Think of something delicious and say mmm!

TASTE

- Taste foods that M, m might like. Say the sound right before you try a bite. You can try Mmmm, munchies, mangoes, or mush.

SMELL

- Choose a scent for N, n. Would they smell like nectarines or noodles?

TOUCH

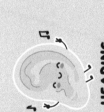

- Touch the N, n in your coloring book. Trace the letter with your fingers.
- Build the letter with letter dough or clay.
- Make the letter in shaving cream or blocks!

MOVEMENT

- Skywrite the letter. Extend your arm with a straight elbow; point your pointer and middle finger and use them to write the letter in the air!
- Lie down on the floor and try to make the letter shapes! Use props if you need them. Have someone take a picture. Look at it and see how you did.

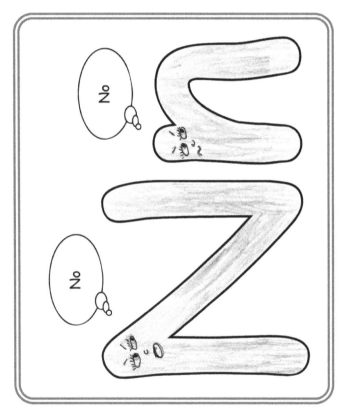

VISION

- Look at N and baby n. Study the shapes.
- Make N, n one color because they only make one sound.
- Make nasty, naughty, negative faces!

HEARING

- Hear the sound nnno!
- Feel how the sound is made with your tongue on the roof of your mouth.
- Shake your head back and forth and make the sound NNN! No!

TASTE

- Taste foods that N, n might like. Say the sound right before you try a bite. You can try noodles, nectarine, nuggets, or nachos.

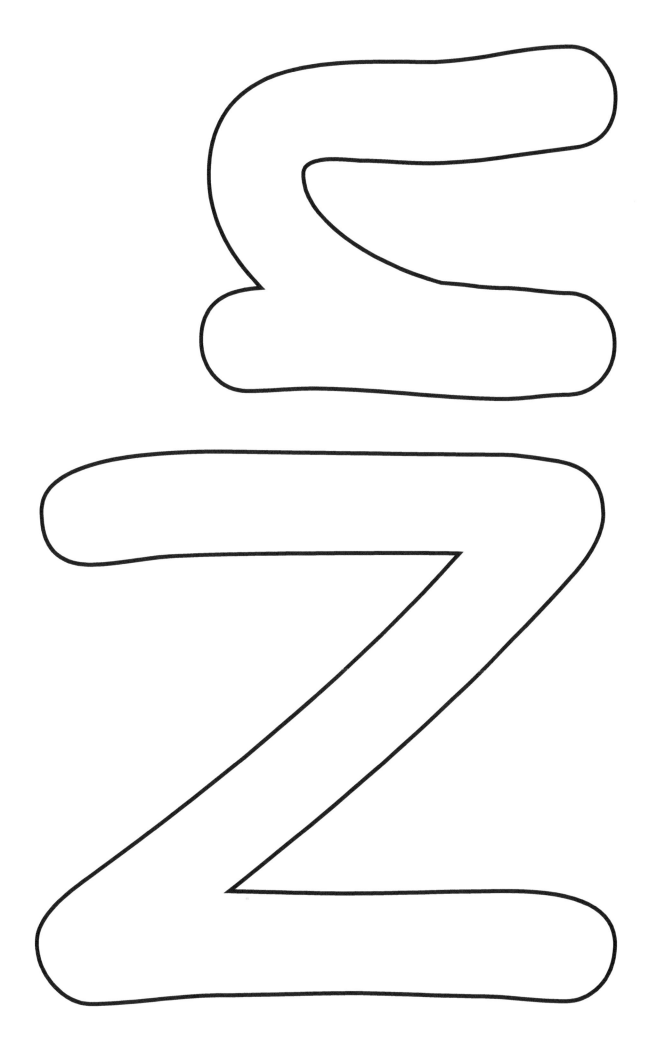

SMELL

- Choose a scent for O, o. Would they smell like olive oil, oatmeal, or oranges?

VISION

- Look at O and baby o. Study the shapes.
- Make them rainbow colors because they are vowels. All vowels have a long sound (their name) and a short sound.
- Make their faces all Os so that they look are surprised! Imagine them saying O and o (aw).

TOUCH

- Touch the O, o in your coloring book. Trace the letter with your fingers.
- Build the letter with letter dough or clay.
- Make the letter in shaving cream or blocks!

HEARING

- Hear the sounds Ō (letter name) and ŏ (Ah... ostrich). "Oh, you have a gift for me! An oostrich!"
- Notice how your mouth makes the shape of an O as you say O and o (ah).
- Put your hand on your neck and feel the vibration in your vocal cords.
- Vowel sounds are made with your vocal cords.

MOVEMENT

- Skywrite the letter. Extend your arm with a straight elbow; point your pointer and middle finger and use them to write the letter in the air!
- Lie down on the floor and try to make the letter shapes! Use props if you need them. Have someone take a picture. Look at it and see how you did.

TASTE

- Taste foods that O, o might like. Say the sound right before you try a bite. You can try oranges, oatmeal, or olives.

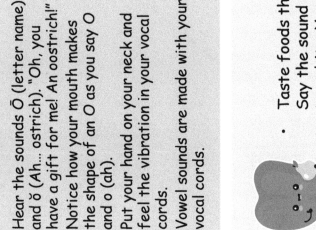

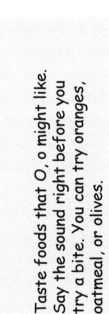

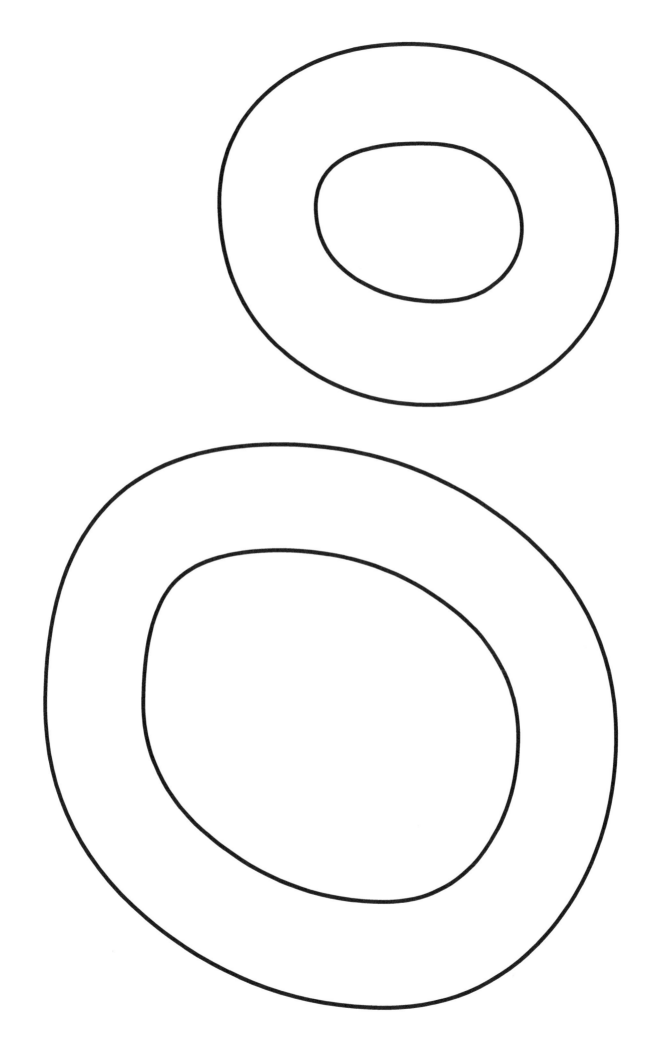

SMELL

- Choose a scent for P, p. Would they smell like peaches, pineapples, or pizza?

VISION

- Look at P and baby p. Study the shapes.
- Make P, p one color because they only make one sound.
- Make their faces look like they need to peel!

TOUCH

- Touch the P, p in your coloring book. Trace the letter with your fingers.
- Build the letter with letter dough or clay.
- Make the letter in shaving cream or blocks!

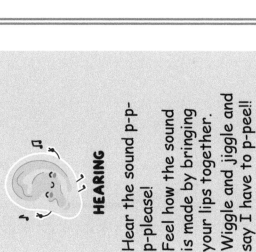

I have to peel!

Oh P!

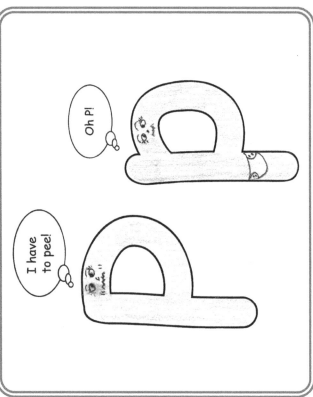

HEARING

- Hear the sound p-p-p-please!
- Feel how the sound is made by bringing your lips together.
- Wiggle and jiggle and say I have to p-peel!

MOVEMENT

- Skywrite the letter. Extend your arm with a straight elbow; point your pointer and middle finger and use them to write the letter in the air!
- Lie down on the floor and try to make the letter shapes! Use props if you need them. Have someone take a picture. Look at it and see how you did.

TASTE

- Taste foods that P, p might like. Say the sound right before you try a bite. You can try peaches, pizza, or pineapples.

SMELL

- Choose a scent for Q, q. Would they smell like quince fruit? A question? What would a question smell like? Maybe they just smell like Q, q? Use your imagination!

TOUCH

- Touch the Q,q in your coloring book. Trace the letter with your fingers.
- Build the letter with letter dough or clay.
- Make the letter in shaving cream or blocks!

MOVEMENT

- Skywrite the letter. Extend your arm with a straight elbow; point your pointer and middle finger and use them to write the letter in the air!
- Lie down on the floor and try to make the letter shapes! Use props if you need them. Have someone take a picture. Look at it and see how you did.

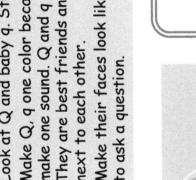

VISION

- Look at Q and baby q. Study the shapes.
- Make Q, q one color because they only make one sound. Q and q love U and u. They are best friends and most always next to each other.
- Make their faces look like they are about to ask a question.

HEARING

- Hear the sound Q-q-q (like kw-kw-kw) question.
- Feel how the sound is made by making a kw sound. You lips round a lot! Like you are going to give a quick kiss.
- Say Q-q-q while making your face look like you have a question!

TASTE

- Taste foods that Q, q might like. Say the sound right before you try a bite. You can try quince fruit or a quart of berries.

VISION

- Look at R and baby r. Study the shapes
- Make R, r one color because they only make one sound.
- Make their faces look like they are ready for anything!
- Draw the things they might put in their pockets to be ready.

SMELL

- Choose a scent for R, r. Would they smell like raspberry or roses?

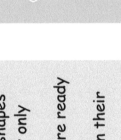

HEARING

- Hear the sound rrready!
- Feel how the sound is made by making a rrrrr sound. This is a complicated sound to make!
- Say Rrrr while you are getting ready!

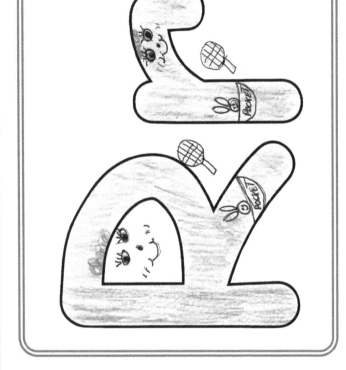

TOUCH

- Touch the R, r in your coloring book. Trace the letter with your fingers.
- Build the letter with letter dough or clay.
- Make the letter in shaving cream or blocks!

MOVEMENT

- Skywrite the letter. Extend your arm with a straight elbow; point your pointer and middle finger and use them to write the letter in the air!
- Lie down on the floor and try to make the letter shapes! Use props if you need them. Have someone take a picture. Look at it and see how you did.

TASTE

- Taste foods that R, r might like. Say the sound right before you try a bite. You can try radishes, rice, raspberries, or raisins.

VISION

- Look at S and baby s. Study the shapes.
- Make S, s two colors because they make two sounds.
- Make their faces look like snake faces.

SMELL

- Choose a scent for S, s. Would they smell like strawberries, sardines, or sugar?

HEARING

- Hear the sound sssnake!
- Feel how the sound is made by making a sss sound. Keep your teeth and lips slightly parted for the sss sound. If you use your vocal cords it turns into a zzz sound.

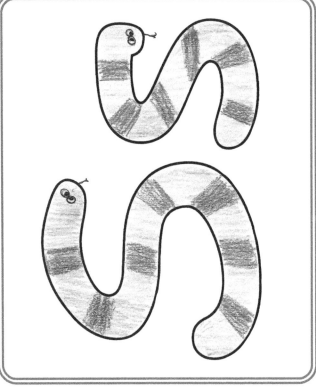

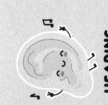

TOUCH

- Touch the S, s in your coloring book. Trace the letter with your fingers.
- Build the letter with letter dough or clay.
- Make the letter in shaving cream or blocks!

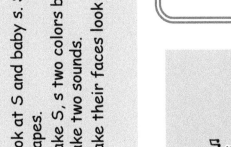

TASTE

- Taste foods that S, s might like. Say the sound right before you try a bite. You can try strawberries, salad, salt, or sugar.

MOVEMENT

- Skywrite the letter. Extend your arm with a straight elbow; point your pointer and middle finger and use them to write the letter in the air!
- Lie down on the floor and try to make the letter shapes! Use props if you need them. Have someone take a picture. Look at it and see how you did.

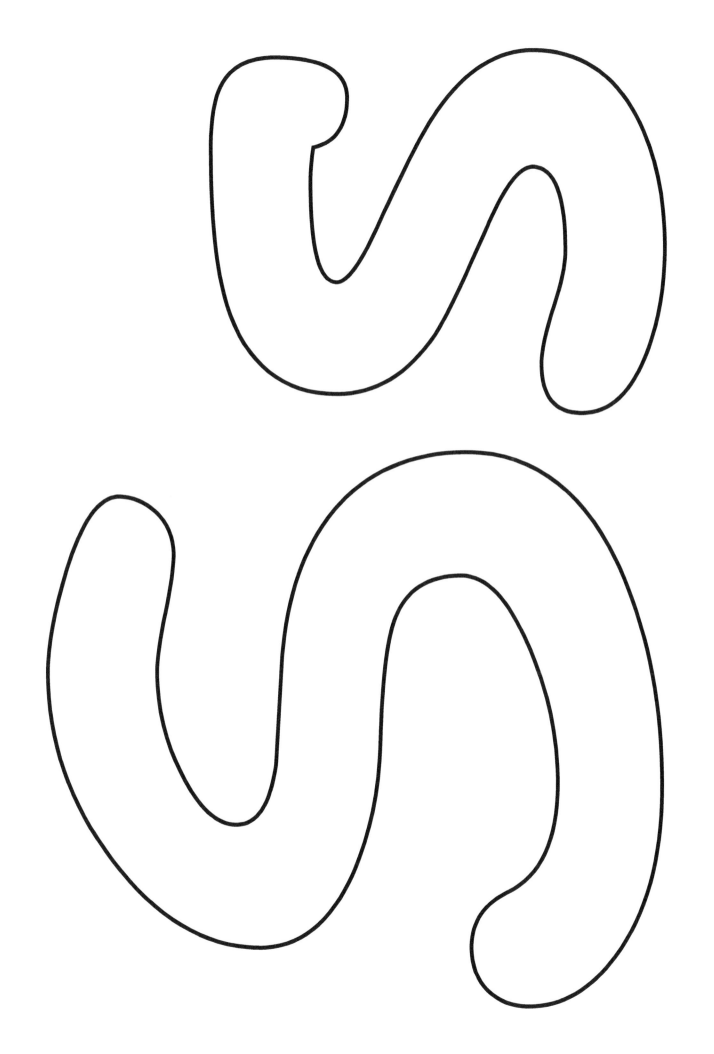

VISION

- Look at T and baby t. Study the shapes.
- Make T, t one color because they make one sounds.
- Make their faces look like they are talking and tipping.

SMELL

- Choose a scent for T, t. Would they smell like tomatoes, tea, or tuna?

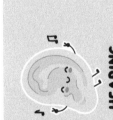

HEARING

- Hear the sound t-t-t-tip.
- Feel how the sound is made by making a ttt sound. Your tongue has to move to release the air to make the sound.
- Say T-t-t while putting your arms out in the t position and tipping to the side.

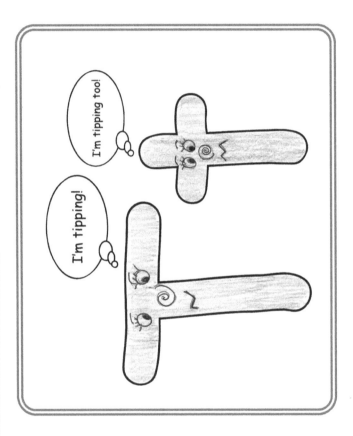

I'm tipping!

I'm tipping too!

TOUCH

- Touch the T, t in your coloring book. Trace the letter with your fingers.
- Build the letter with letter dough or clay.
- Make the letter in shaving cream or blocks!

MOVEMENT

- Skywrite the letter. Extend your arm with a straight elbow; point your pointer and middle finger and use them to write the letter in the air!
- Lie down on the floor and try to make the letter shapes! Use props if you need them. Have someone take a picture. Look at it and see how you did.

TASTE

- Taste foods that T, t might like. Say the sound right before you try a bite. You can try tomatoes, tea, tuna, or turkey.

SMELL

- Choose a scent for U, u. Would they smell like upside-down cake?

TOUCH

- Touch the U, u in your coloring book. Trace the letter with your fingers.
- Build the letter with letter dough or clay.
- Make the letter in shaving cream or blocks!

MOVEMENT

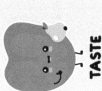

- Skywrite the letter. Extend your arm with a straight elbow; point your pointer and middle finger and use them to write the letter in the air!
- Lie down on the floor and try to make the letter shapes! Use props if you need them. Have someone take a picture. Look at it and see how you did.

VISION

- Look at U and baby u. Study the shapes.
- Make them rainbow colors because they are vowels. All vowels have a long sound (their name) and a short sound!
- Make their faces look unselfish and understanding!

HEARING

- Hear the sounds Ū (letter name) and ŭ (up, umbrella, mule like an oo sound).
- Say, "Hey, U, do you need a unique umbrella?" All vowels have a long sound, their name, and a short sound (u has two short sounds – u as in umbrella and u as in mule oo)!
- Put your hand on your neck and feel the vibration in your vocal cords.
- Vowel sounds are made with your vocal cords.

TASTE

- Taste foods that U, u might like. Say the sound right before you try a bite. You can try umbrella fruit or upside-down cake.

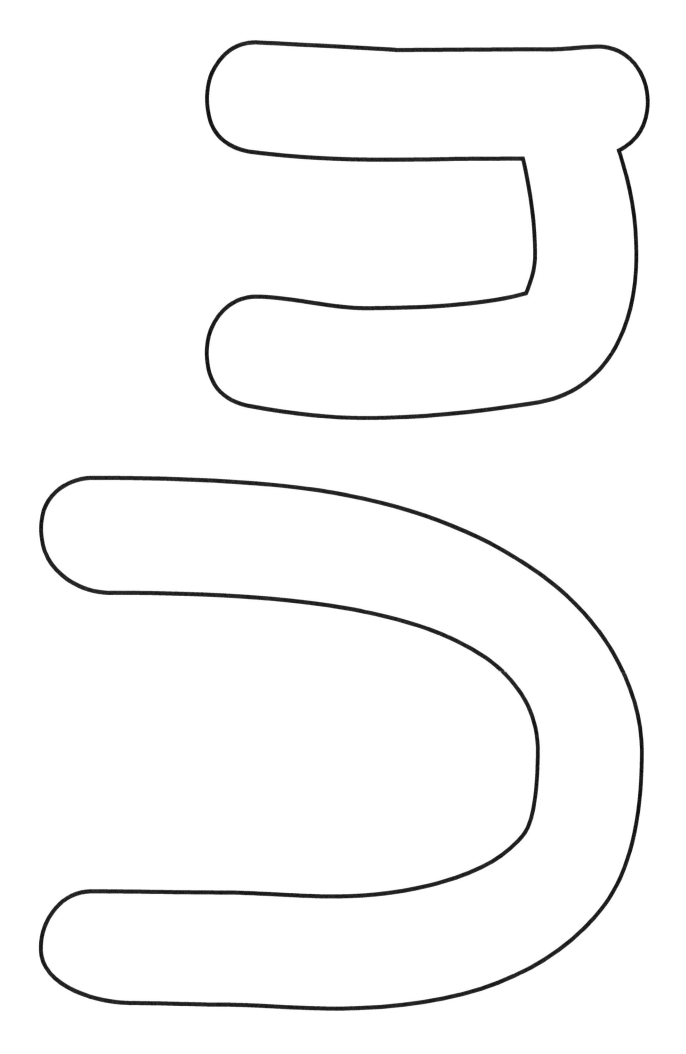

SMELL

- Choose a scent for V, v. Would they smell like vanilla or vinegar?

TOUCH

- Touch the V, v in your coloring book. Trace the letter with your fingers.
- Build the letter with letter dough or clay.
- Make the letter in shaving cream or blocks!

MOVEMENT

- Skywrite the letter. Extend your arm with a straight elbow; point your pointer and middle finger and use them to write the letter in the air!
- Lie down on the floor and try to make the letter shapes! Use props if you need them. Have someone take a picture. Look at it and see how you did.

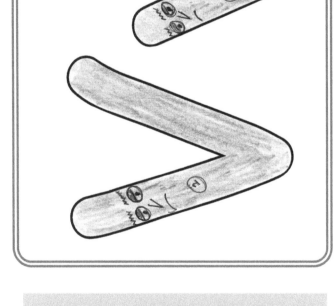

VISION

- Look at V and baby v. Study the shapes.
- Make V, v one color because they make one sound.
- Make their faces look like vicious.

HEARING

- Hear the sound vvvillain! Feel how the sound is made when you put your top teeth on your bottom lip and blow – vvv.
- Say V-v-v while raising your hands in a V for Victory.

TASTE

- Taste foods that V, v might like. Say the sound right before you try a bite. You can try vegetables, vinegar, or vanilla (ice cream).

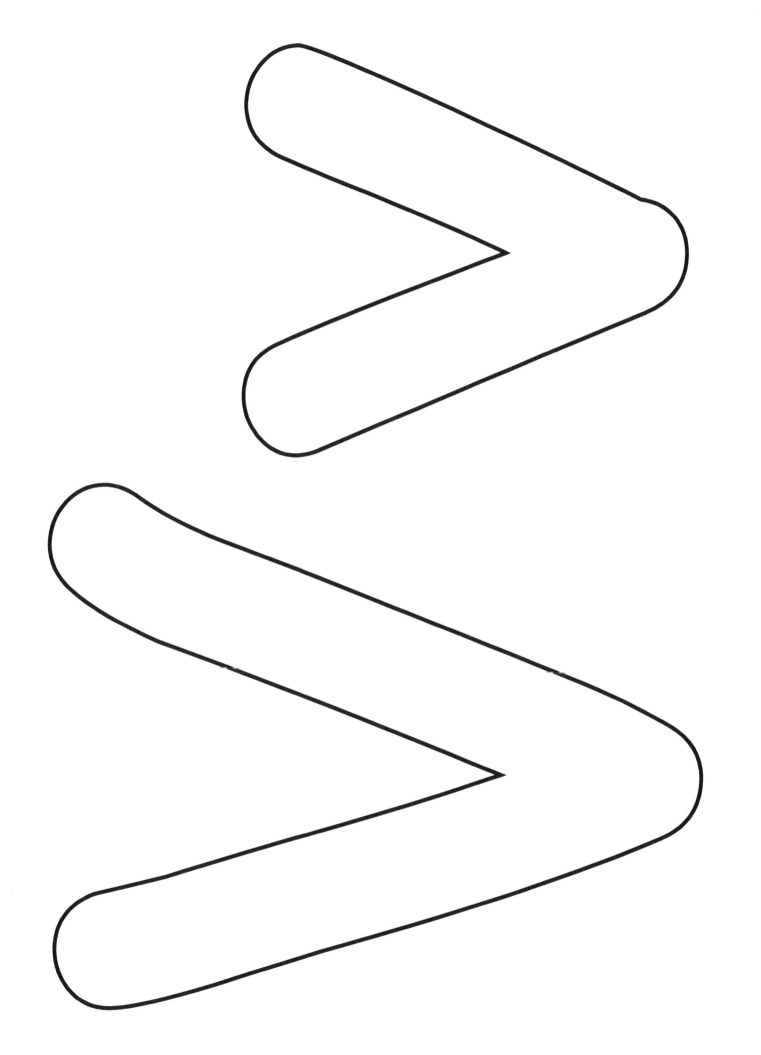

VISION

- Look at W and baby w. Study the shapes.
- Make W, w one color because they make one sound.
- Make them look wavy and watery.

SMELL

- Choose a scent for W, w. Would they smell like watermelon?

TOUCH

- Touch the W, w in your coloring book. Trace the letter with your fingers.
- Build the letter with letter dough or clay.
- Make the letter in shaving cream or blocks!

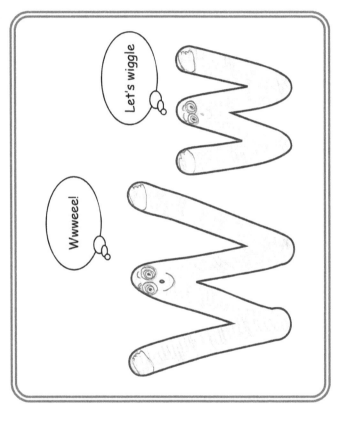

Wwweee!

Let's wiggle

MOVEMENT

- Skywrite the letter. Extend your arm with a straight elbow; point your pointer and middle finger and use them to write the letter in the air!
- Lie down on the floor and try to make the letter shapes! Use props if you need them. Have someone take a picture. Look at it and see how you did.

HEARING

- Hear the sound W, w! W-w-water.
- Feel how the sound is made by rounding your lips w-w-w. Notice how your jaw and lips move when you make the sound.
- Say w-w-w while listening to water run.

TASTE

- Taste foods that W, w might like. Say the sound right before you try a bite. You can try wontons, watermelon, or wieners.

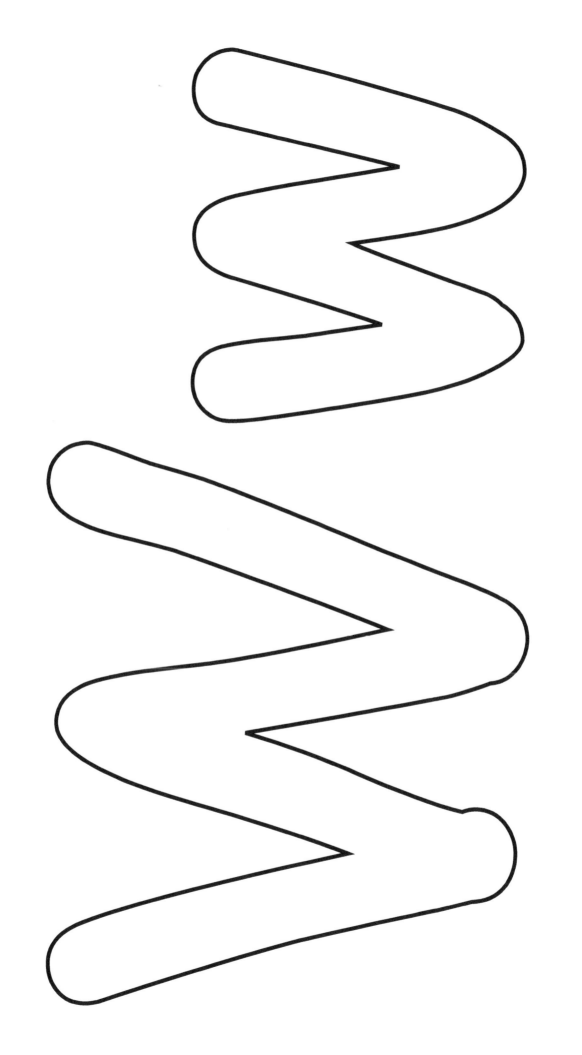

SMELL

- Choose a scent for X, x. Get creative on this one. Ask your little one, to come up with something they think X would smell like!

TOUCH

- Touch the X, x in your coloring book. Trace the letter with your fingers.
- Build the letter with letter dough or clay.
- Make the letter in shaving cream or blocks!

VISION

- Look at X and baby x. Study the shapes.
- Make X, x two colors because they make two sounds. (X-Ray, Ax, ks sound, X can also sound like Z, but you can teach that later - Xylophone- z sound).
- Focus mostly on the ks sound.
- Make their eyes look like they have X-Ray vision.

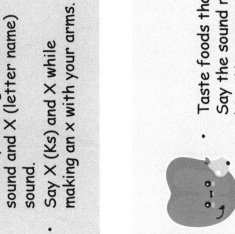

I see inside with my x-ray vision.

Want to play jax?

HEARING

- Hear the sounds X, x-x-x... ks, ks, ks.
- Feel how the sounds are made by making the x (ks) sound and X (letter name) sound.
- Say X (Ks) and X while making an x with your arms.

MOVEMENT

- Skywrite the letter. Extend your arm with a straight elbow; point your pointer and middle finger and use them to write the letter in the air!
- Lie down on the floor and try to make the letter shapes! Use props if you need them. Have someone take a picture. Look at it and see how you did.

TASTE

- Taste foods that X, x might like. Say the sound right before you try a bite. You can try X shaped cookies?

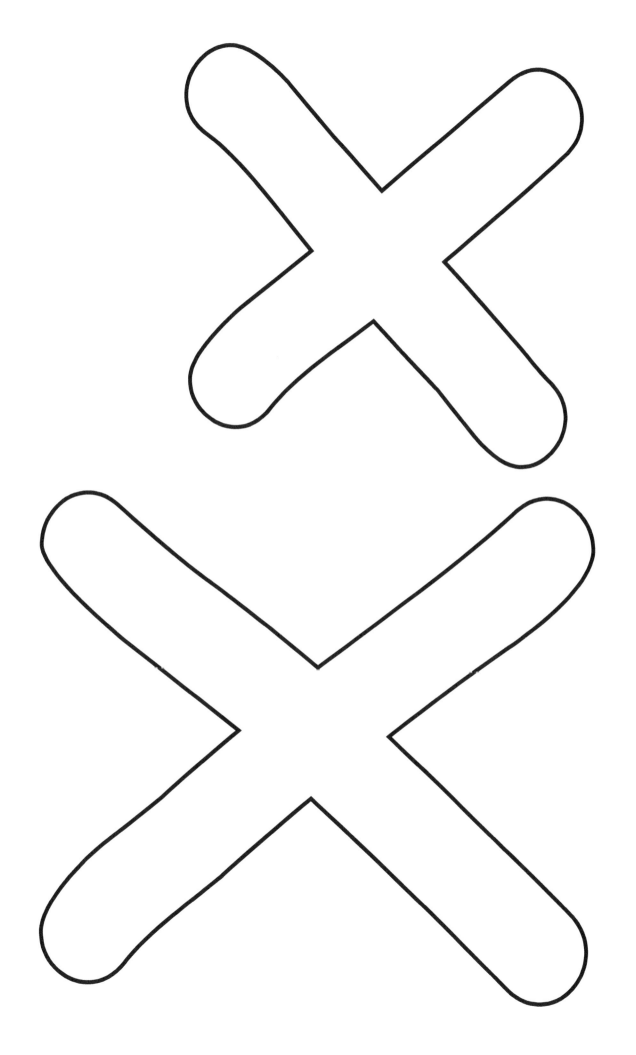

VISION

- Look at Y and baby y. Study the shapes. Make Y, y half rainbow because Y can be a vowel (by long i sound, baby - long e sound) and half one color because he can be a consonant (yellow).
- Make their faces look happy like they are saying yes!

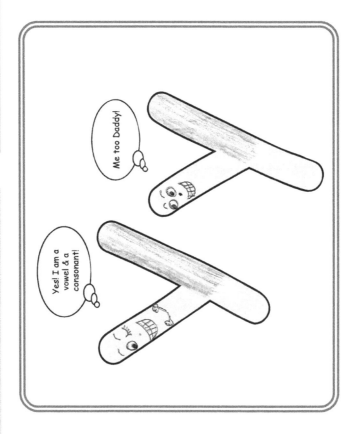

Yes! I am a vowel & a consonant!

Me too Daddy!

SMELL

- Choose a scent for Y, y. Would they smell like yams or yolks?

TOUCH

- Touch the Y, y in your coloring book. Trace the letter with your fingers.
- Build the letter with letter dough or clay.
- Make the letter in shaving cream or blocks!

MOVEMENT

- Skywrite the letter. Extend your arm with a straight elbow; point your pointer and middle finger and use them to write the letter in the air!
- Lie down on the floor and try to make the letter shapes! Use props if you need them. Have someone take a picture. Look at it and see how you did.

HEARING

- Hear the sounds Y, y-y-yes! (Focus on the consonant sound and mention that y can sound like E or I.)
- Feel how the sound is made by making Yyy sound. Notice how your tongue moves.
- Say Y (as in Yes) while nodding your head yes!

TASTE

- Taste foods that Y, y might like. Say the sound right before you try a bite. You can try yams, yokes, or yogurt.

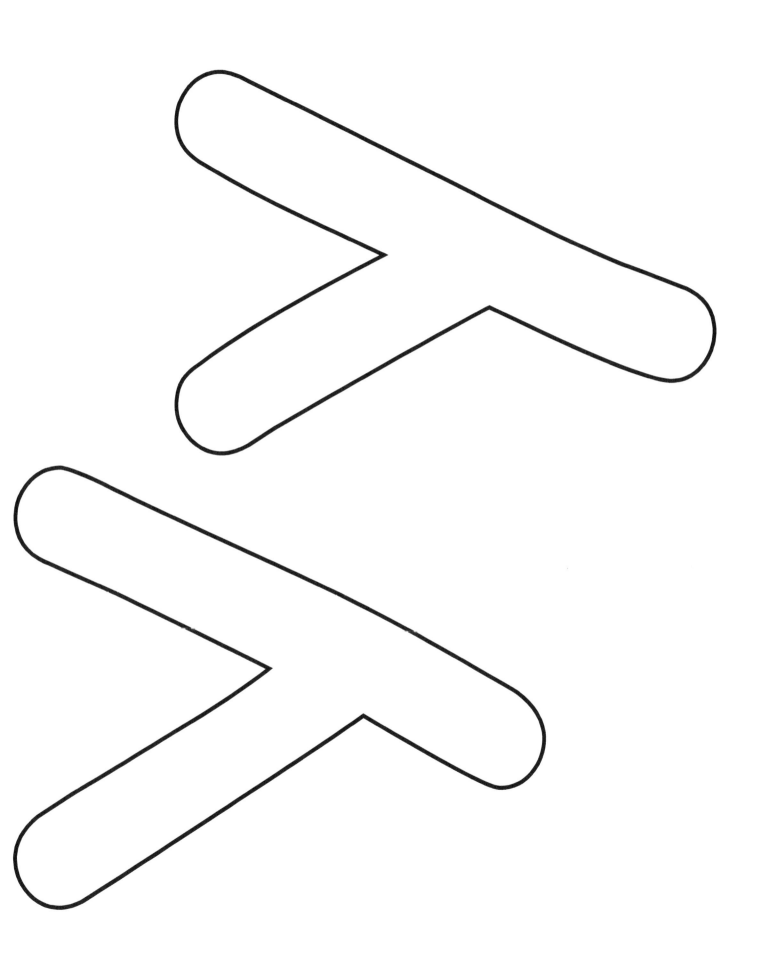

SMELL

- Choose a scent for Z, z. Would they smell like (lemon) zest?

VISION

- Look at Z and baby z. Study the shapes.
- Make Z, z one color because Z has one sound.
- Make them look like they are zooming and zipping.

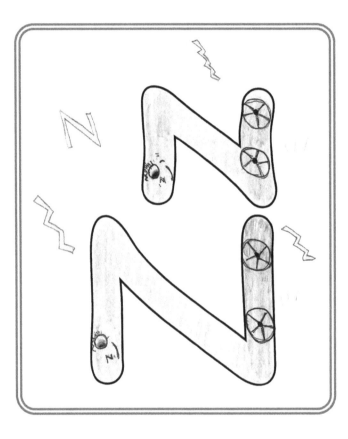

TOUCH

- Touch the Z, z in your coloring book. Trace the letter with your fingers.
- Build the letter with letter dough or clay.
- Make the letter in shaving cream or blocks!

HEARING

- Hear the sound zzzzip!
- Feel how the sound buzzes in your mouth.
- Say Zzzzzz while zooming around.

MOVEMENT

- Skywrite the letter. Extend your arm with a straight elbow; point your pointer and middle finger and use them to write the letter in the air!
- Lie down on the floor and try to make the letter shapes! Use props if you need them. Have someone take a picture. Look at it and see how you did.

TASTE

- Taste foods that Z, z might like. Say the sound right before you try a bite. You can try ziti, zucchini, zeppole.

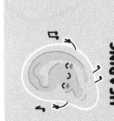

SIGHT WORDS

Sight words or high frequency words make up about 75 percent of beginning books for children. These words sometimes do not follow letter pattern/phonics rules and are not decoded or tapped out. They are memorized and recognized like pictures or logos. Included here, are the first group for your child to learn. Once they know these and their letter sounds, they will be ready to start reading decodable books!

To teach these words, first say the word while using your pointer and middle finger of the hand that you write with to trace a line in the direction of the arrow under the word. Next have your child do the same. Repeat this see-and-say exercise.

Next try spell reading. Do the previous exercise and add this step... Ask your little reader to spell the word after they say it. For example, have them say "the" as they underline the word with their finger. Next have them spell "t-h-e" as they underline the word with their finger and after they spell it have them say it again (the, t-h-e, the).

Have your child skywrite the word.

You can also have them sing sight words - first singing the sight word, then singing/spelling it, then singing/saying it.

Have your child color these sight words in the coloring activity book.

Review the words and check the boxes below them to indicate when your child has read the word ten times without hesitation. Then you can call that word a graduate!

Check the boxes below each time the word is read without hesitation.

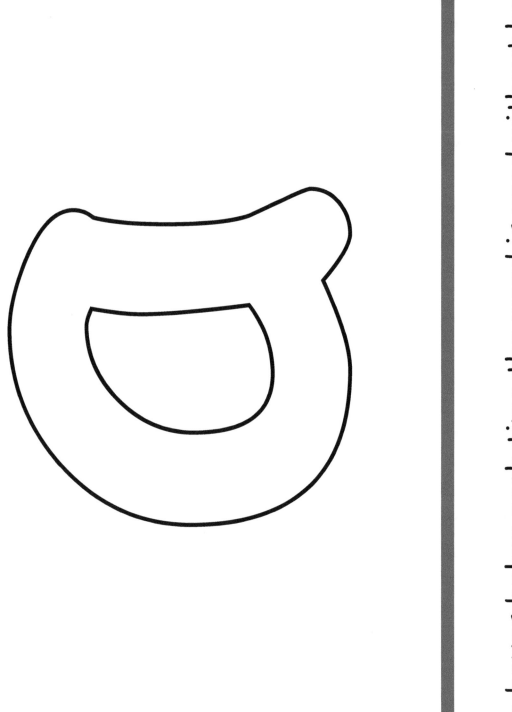

Check the boxes below each time the word is read without hesitation.

Check the boxes below each time the word is read without hesitation.

Check the boxes below each time the word is read without hesitation.

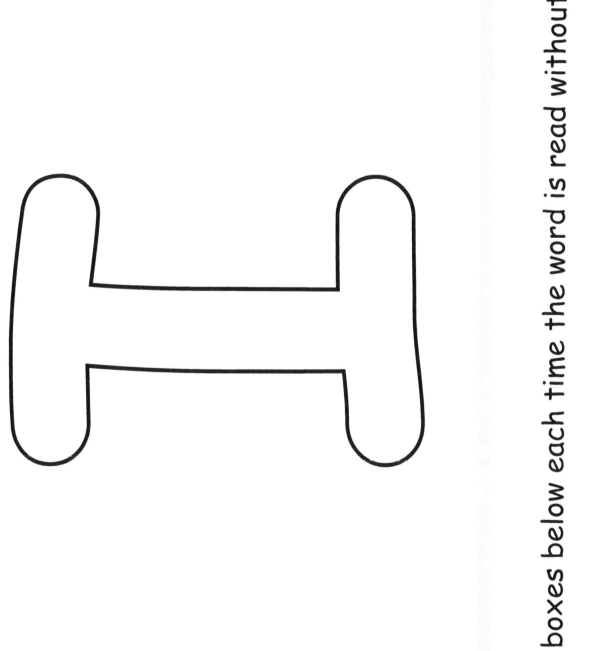

Check the boxes below each time the word is read without hesitation.

Check the boxes below each time the word is read without hesitation.

Check the boxes below each time the word is read without hesitation.

Check the boxes below each time the word is read without hesitation.

Check the boxes below each time the word is read without hesitation.

into

Check the boxes below each time the word is read without hesitation.

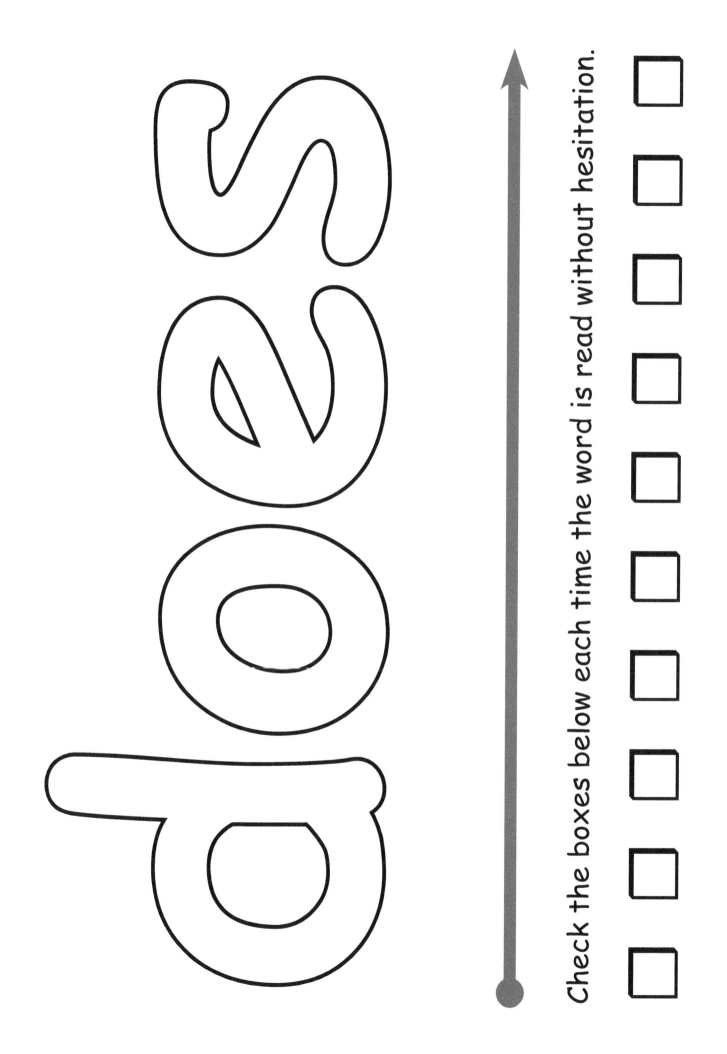

does

Check the boxes below each time the word is read without hesitation.

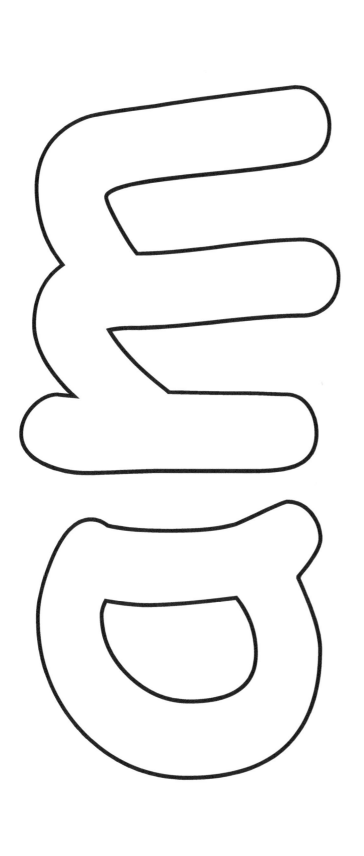

Check the boxes below each time the word is read without hesitation.

CPSIA information can be obtained
at www.ICGtesting.com
Printed in the USA
BVHW061310301220
596702BV00002B/16